Abigail Adams

★ ★ ★ Eyewitness to ★ ★ ★ America's Birth

By the Editors of TIME For Kids
WITH RACHEL ORR

Collins
An Imprint of HarperCollinsPublishers

About the Author: Rachel Orr is a freelance writer, editor, and literary agent. She has also worked at the American Embassy in London's Grosvenor Square, where Abigail Adams once lived. Rachel resides with her husband in Hoboken, New Jersey.

Collins is an imprint of HarperCollins Publishers.
Abigail Adams
Copyright © 2009 by Time Inc.
Used under exclusive license by HarperCollins Publishers Inc.
Manufactured in China.

Library of Congress Cataloging-in-Publication Data is available.
ISBN 978-0-06-057628-8 (pbk.) — ISBN 978-0-06-057629-5 (trade)

1 2 3 4 5 6 7 8 9 10
First Edition

J 973.4
A81

4-28-10

Copyright © by Time Inc.

TIME FOR KIDS and the Red Border Design are Trademarks of Time Inc. used under license.

Photography and Illustration Credits:
Cover: Hulton Archive/Getty Images; inset: courtesy of the Massachusetts Historical Society; front flap: The Bridgeman Art Library/Getty Images; title page: Adams National Historical Park, National Park Service ; (flag background) National Geographic RF Collection/Fotosearch; contents page: The Massachusetts Historical Society/The Bridgeman Art Library; p. iv: Adams National Historical Park, National Park Service ; p. 1: HIP/Art Resource; p. 2: Hulton Archive/Getty Images; p. 3: The Granger Collection, New York; p. 4: courtesy of Abigail Adams Historical Society; p. 5: (top) Print Collection, Miriam and Ira D. Wallach Division of Art, Prints and Photographs, The New York Public Library; p. 5: (bottom) The Granger Collection, New York; pp. 6, 7, 8: (4) The Granger Collection, New York; p. 9: (top) The Massachusetts Historical Society/The Bridgeman Art Library; p. 9 (bottom): The Granger Collection, New York ; p. 10: The New York Public Library/Art Resource; p. 11: (top left) The Art Archive/Culver Pictures; p. 11 (top right): Musee de l'Assistance Publique, Hopitaux de Paris, France/ Archives Charmet/ The Bridgeman Art Library; pp. 12, 13: (3) The Granger Collection, New York; p. 14: Library of Congress, Prints and Photographs Division, 3b52116; p. 15: Hulton Archive/Getty Images; p. 16: Private Collection/The Bridgeman Art Library; p. 17: Getty Images; p. 19 (top and bottom): (2) The Granger Collection, New York; p. 20: Time & Life Pictures/Getty Images; p. 21: Hulton Archive/Getty Images; p. 22: (top) North Wind Picture Archives; p. 22 (bottom):Abigail Adams to John Adams, 16 October 1774. Original manuscript from the Adams family papers. Courtesy of the Massachusetts Historical Society; p. 23: North Wind Picture Archives; pp. 24-27: (3) The Granger Collection, New York; p. 28: Stapleton Collection/Corbis; p. 29: Mary Evans Picture Library; p. 30: North Wind Picture Archives; p. 31: The Granger Collection, New York; p. 32: Adams National Historical Park, National Park Service; p. 33: The Granger Collection, New York; pp. 34, 35: The Art Archive/Private Collection/Gianni Dagli Orti; p. 36: The Granger Collection, New York; p. 37: AP Images/Susan Walsh; p. 38: (left) Newscom; p.38 (right): Library of Congress, Prints and Photographs Division, 3g05801; p. 39: Hulton Archive/Getty Images; p. 40 (top)): Adams National Historical Park, National Park Service; p. 40 (bottom): The Library of Congress, Prints and Photographs Division, 3b04519; p. 41: The Granger Collection, New York; p. 42: courtesy of Kelly Cobble; p. 43: Michael Smith/ Newsmakers/Getty Images; p. 44 (top to bottom): Hulton Archive/Getty Images; Time & Life Pictures/Getty Images; The Bridgeman Art Library/ Getty Images; back cover: Adams National Historical Park, National Park Service

Acknowledgments:
For TIME FOR KIDS: Art Director: ShapiroDesign; Photography Editor: Stacey D'Alessi; Editor: Curtis Slepian

 Find out more at www.timeforkids.com/bio/adams

CONTENTS

"... in the new Code of Laws which I suppose it will be necessary for you to make I desire you would Remember the Ladies ..."

—ABIGAIL ADAMS

REMEMBER
the Ladies

On July 18, 1776, a crowd gathered in front of the State House in Boston, Massachusetts. Everyone was waiting for the officials to read an important announcement. It was called the Declaration of Independence. The thirteen American colonies did not want to be ruled by Britain anymore. They wanted to announce their freedom.

Abigail Adams was inspired by the Declaration of Independence, although she knew the colonists would have to continue fighting for their freedom.

▲ **A CROWD** heard the Declaration of Independence read at the State House in Boston, Massachusetts. "Every face appeared joyful," said Abigail.

The Revolutionary War, which had started in 1775, would last for seven more years. Abigail knew that women would have to fight for their rights too. Four months earlier, Abigail had written to her husband, John Adams, asking him to "remember the ladies" when making new laws for the country. She wasn't asking for the right to vote, but she *did* want fairer laws—such as allowing women to keep some of the money they earned, instead of giving it to their husbands.

John laughed at her wish. Yet Abigail went on to play an important role in the new nation. She took care of their home and children while her husband was in Europe making peace treaties with other countries.

Years later, in a role that would become known as "First Lady," she helped President Adams make important decisions. Abigail had always been a woman with her own opinions. She had started speaking her mind long before, when she was a young girl in Weymouth, Massachusetts.

NEW YORKERS tear down a statue of King George III in Manhattan in 1776. It was melted into bullets that were later used by the Continental Army.

CHAPTER 2

ABIGAIL'S
Admirable Family

◄ VISITORS can see Abigail's birthplace in Weymouth, Massachusetts. Built in 1685, the house has been restored.

Abigail was born on October 11, 1744, in Weymouth. This was a small seaside town in the Massachusetts Bay Colony, surrounded by forest and farmland.

Most men in Weymouth were farmers. But Abigail's father, William Smith, was a minister. He preached at the North Parish Congregational Church. There he baptized his four children—Mary, Abigail, Billy, and

Betsey. William had a degree from Harvard College, and he loved to read. A generous man, he loaned books to the many men who visited his home library.

Abigail's mother, Elizabeth Quincy Smith, was also well respected in the community. Although she could be cold and distant, she took good care of the sick and the poor. Sometimes Abigail would go with her mother on these visits. She learned that women had an important role helping their neighbors and family.

As a child, Abigail (called "Nabby") was shy. She was also very stubborn. Abigail listened to her parents but knew how to get her own way. Elizabeth often sent Abigail to stay with her Grandmother Quincy, who understood Abigail completely.

► GIRLS like Abigail learned to sew and take care of the house.

The two were very fond of each other.

Growing up, Abigail spent more time with relatives than friends. Since she was frequently sick and had to stay indoors, her sisters were her closest playmates. When she was well, Abigail loved visiting her Uncle Isaac and Aunt Elizabeth in Boston. And she adored Dr. Cotton Tufts, a cousin who lived nearby. They remained close their entire lives.

A Love for Learning

While their brother, Billy, went to school, Abigail and her sisters were educated at home. At that time, girls learned only what they needed to know to take care of a home and family. Elizabeth helped her daughters with their ABCs and numbers. She also showed them how to sew. When the girls were older,

▲ COLONIAL kids used hornbooks to learn to read. They were lesson sheets covered by thin cow horn.

William taught them literature and history. Abigail often read from her father's library and loved to quote poetry.

Although Abigail learned a lot, she knew that she was not as well educated as a boy. Her handwriting and spelling were poor. This embarrassed Abigail as she grew older. She felt that since women were responsible for teaching their children, they should be better educated. So Abigail fought for women's education her entire life.

▼ **THE NEW ENGLAND PRIMER** was a textbook Abigail probably read.

Church Manners

The Pilgrims were the first Congregationalists in Massachusetts. They arrived from England in 1620 with lots of strict rules. In the mid-1700s, families sat through Sunday service for nine hours, with only a short lunch break. After lunch, a man was paid to make sure that no one fell asleep. He carried a rod with a feather on one end. If a woman was caught sleeping, she would get tickled with the feather. A man, however, would get hit with the rod! These "common sleepers" were often fined and shunned by the community. It was very important to keep your eyes open in church.

3

PARTNERS
for Life

As a teenager, Abigail sometimes studied with Richard Cranch, who often visited her sister Mary. One summer day in 1759, Richard brought along a friend named John Adams. Abigail did not like John at first. The twenty-three-year-old lawyer was short, overweight, and talked too much. John was not very impressed with Abigail either. He thought the fourteen-year-old was funny and clever, but not very graceful.

Over the next few years, Abigail got to know John better. She discovered they

◄ JOHN ADAMS in 1766. This is the earliest painting of Abigail's husband.

had a lot in common, including a sense of humor. Abigail liked John's ambition. He liked the fact that she was educated. Whenever he could, John rode his horse five miles from his Braintree home to see her. By 1762, the couple was planning a wedding.

Abigail wanted to get married in the spring. Unfortunately, nearly seven hundred people in Boston came down with smallpox—an illness that could be deadly. The wedding would have to wait.

Since John traveled to Boston for work, he decided to be inoculated. (This is like getting a shot to prevent disease. In those days, it was a risky treatment—

▲ A DOCTOR inoculates a baby against smallpox, a deadly disease.

some people died from the side effects.) Abigail also wanted to be inoculated, but her mother said no. Sadly, the couple was separated for three weeks. They missed each other and wrote lots of letters.

John and Abigail were finally married on October 25, 1764. Abigail's father performed the ceremony at home. That day marked the beginning of a marriage built on trust and friendship. They would be partners for life.

Happy Marriage

After their wedding, the couple moved into a small farmhouse in Braintree. They grew fruit and vegetables, and raised cows, chickens, and sheep. Since they lived near the

▲ **ABIGAIL AND JOHN** lived in this farmhouse in Braintree, Massachusetts. Here, John practiced law and co-wrote the Massachusetts Constitution.

seashore, they could get fresh fish at the market too. John and Abigail were lucky that they could

A Shot in the Arm

▲ NABBY ADAMS was Abigail's first child and her favorite. Nabby helped her mother with chores around the house.

afford to eat meat every day. Most families could not. Also, Abigail could buy fabrics and soap in nearby Boston instead of making them herself.

Even though Abigail saw her family often, she was still lonely. John traveled a lot for work. And taking a carriage out during the winter was difficult. Yet she soon had someone to keep her

When people caught smallpox, their bodies were covered in blisters. This sounds like chicken pox, but it was much more dangerous. Smallpox killed millions of people—especially American Indians—in the 1700s.

John Adams's great-uncle, Dr. Zabdiel Boylston, first inoculated the colonists. He put pus from a smallpox blister into his patients' skin. They would then get a mild case of smallpox and never catch it again. Since the disease was easily spread, patients had to be kept apart from their friends and family for several weeks.

People don't catch smallpox anymore. Thanks to modern medicine, we don't have to worry about getting this terrible disease.

company. A daughter, Abigail (also called "Nabby," like her mother), was born in July 1765.

Trouble with Britain

Around the time Nabby was born, Boston citizens were angry. Parliament, the British lawmaking

body that ruled the American colonies, had passed the Stamp Act. This act forced Americans to pay taxes on newspapers, playing cards, and other documents. Since they weren't allowed to have a representative in Parliament, the colonists thought the tax was unfair. Many shouted, "No taxation without representation!" Americans made sure their voices were heard about this—loud and clear.

The people of Boston were especially angry. They protested the tax by attacking

◄ COLONISTS protested against the Stamp Act. They thought it was unfair that Britain could tax their products.

the home of the British tax collector. In 1766 Parliament got rid of the Stamp Act because it was too difficult to enforce. Celebrations were held in Boston, but they wouldn't last for long. Parliament was keeping a close eye on Boston, and there would only be more trouble in the months to come.

MOBS in Boston and other cities attacked stamp officers. Many of the officers resigned in fear.

LIFE IN
Boston

In 1768 the Adams family moved to Boston. Abigail loved living in the city, which was six times bigger than Braintree. The streets were crowded and noisy, but Abigail didn't mind. She liked to watch the ships

▲ **BOSTON HARBOR** was the hub of trade in New England in the 1700s.

in the harbor and read the papers while the news was still fresh. (By the time a paper got to Braintree, the news was several days old.) She also liked listening to John

and his friends discuss politics. Even though it wasn't considered a proper subject for women, Abigail had her own opinions.

Abigail was also very busy raising her children. This was an important duty, which she took very seriously. She read lots of books on the subject and wrote to friends for advice. The couple now had three children: Nabby, John Quincy, and Susanna (called "Suky"). Sadly, Suky died in 1770 when she was thirteen months old. Abigail was devastated. Toddler deaths were not unusual back then, but this was still a difficult time for Abigail.

Soon after the Adams family had moved to Boston, British soldiers arrived to keep peace. However, peace would not last for long. On March 5, 1770, Abigail heard shouts outside. She saw the shadows of soldiers rushing down the dark street. John was still at a meeting, and Abigail worried that he was in danger.

When John finally arrived home, he told her the news: A large group of men had been throwing snowballs and oyster shells at the British soldiers. Suddenly, somebody yelled "Fire!" and the soldiers

THE BOSTON MASSACRE made the colonists angry at the British.

shot into the crowd. Five American colonists were killed. This event would become known as the Boston Massacre. It turned more colonists against British rule.

The next few years were quiet for the Adams family, which was growing quickly. Charles was born in 1770, and another son, Thomas, was born two years later. It was also a mostly peaceful time for the colonies—until 1773, when Parliament decided to tax any tea shipped to America. Tea was a popular drink, so people were angry. Abigail was curious to see what would happen when the ships arrived in Boston Harbor. It turned out to be a historic event: On a December night, a group of men dressed up like American Indians snuck onto the three ships and threw 342 chests of tea into

the water. Parliament closed the harbor until the colonists paid for the tea. (They never did.)

◄ THE BOSTON TEA PARTY got colonists in hot water: Angry England shut down the local government.

During the Boston Tea Party, Abigail was visiting her parents in Weymouth. She wrote to John and begged to know the details. When she heard about the rebellion, she was thrilled, although she worried about what would happen next. The colonies were quickly losing their rights, and the future didn't look so promising. Abigail anxiously concluded that the next step might be war.

Abigail wrote to her friend Mercy Otis Warren about the tea party. The two women often sent each other letters.

▲ MERCY OTIS WARREN was a published writer.

Mercy was sixteen years older than Abigail and taught her a lot about life and politics. Abigail would need Mercy's support during the following years, since she would be home alone without her husband.

In the summer of 1774, John was chosen to serve in the Continental Congress. Representatives from the colonies would meet in Philadelphia to decide how to unite against Britain. Abigail and the children moved back to Braintree. They would stay there for the many war-torn years to come.

The REVOLUTION Begins

Abigail had to make a lot of important decisions while John was in Philadelphia. As time passed, she grew even more confident in her abilities. She took care of the farm and managed John's law practice. She also hired a tutor for seven-year-old John Quincy and taught the other children at home. Schools were closed, since war was such a huge threat. Abigail worried constantly. One day, she watched a group of colonists steal British gunpowder. Abigail feared war would come soon.

She was right. On April 19, 1775, troops fought the Battle of Lexington and Concord.

This was the first battle in the American Revolutionary War. The fight was only twenty miles from Abigail's home. But now she was too busy to be worried. She housed people escaping the British in

▲ **THE FIRST BATTLE** of the American Revolution was fought in Concord and Lexington on April 19, 1775. This handbill (left), listing the casualties of the battle, was published soon after.

Boston. She melted pewter utensils to make musket balls for the American soldiers training in her yard. Abigail wrote to John, saying, "You can hardly imagine how we live."

John shared Abigail's reports with the Continental Congress. They were deciding if America should break away from Britain. Their decision was very important to the people of Boston. However, Congress didn't know how difficult it was for their fellow colonists to live surrounded by soldiers. Abigail's words helped them to understand the danger.

▲ ABIGAIL witnessed from a distance the bloody Battle of Bunker Hill.

Abigail was a key witness to battle as well. On the morning of June 17, 1775, she woke to the firing of cannons. With young John Quincy, she ran to the top of a nearby hill and watched as Charlestown burned across the river. The Battle of Bunker Hill raged all day. Later, Abigail learned that the colonists had lost that fight. She also learned that a family friend, Dr. Joseph Warren, had been killed.

As the war continued, Abigail knew that she was ready to be free from Britain. She refused to join in her church's prayers for peace. Finally, on July 4, 1776, the Continental Congress approved the Declaration of Independence. The proclamation was read in several cities. Abigail heard it in Boston, where she had gone with the children to be inoculated from smallpox. (She didn't tell John.) The procedure was far worse than Abigail had expected. John was upset when he found out, yet Abigail kept him updated on everyone's health.

The Long Separation Continues

Although the troops had moved on to New York, times were still hard in Braintree. Prices were high, so Abigail and her friends worked together to sew their own clothes. They also made "liberty tea" out of leaves from their gardens. This way, they wouldn't have to buy

clothes and tea from Britain. The women were proud of their American products.

Even though Abigail was good at taking care of the farm and children while John was away, she wished he could come home. However, she soon learned that he'd be gone even

▶ IN ABIGAIL'S time, people sailed to Europe in schooners.

Special Delivery!

A bigail and John wrote more than one thousand letters to each other. (Remember, there were no telephones or computers in the 1700s!) And, as Abigail wrote in one letter to her husband, "My pen is always freer than my tongue. I have wrote many things to you that I suppose I never could have talked."

In her letters, Abigail described the details of her life during the American Revolution. She told about the struggles of running a home with wartime shortages and rising costs. She wrote about running the farm with little help and finding time to educate her children. And mostly, Abigail wrote to John about her loneliness without him.

◀ OF THE LETTERS that Abigail and John wrote to each other, about 1,200 survive. This is one of them.

longer: Congress wanted him to go to Paris and ask for France's support in the war. Abigail was upset. Yet, as always, she knew this was an important way for John to serve his country in the fight for independence. They believed it was worth the sacrifice of living far apart.

Abigail wanted to go to Paris, too, but John said the trip was too difficult for a woman. So they decided that John Quincy should go instead. It would be a terrific opportunity for the ten-year-old boy to study French and learn about a new culture.

In February 1778, John and John Quincy sailed to Europe. Abigail was so sad that she couldn't even go to the shore to watch them leave.

Sending those letters was not as easy as it is today. Colonial mail was first delivered in 1673, when a postman rode on horseback from New York to Boston. The trip took two weeks. Eighty years later, Benjamin Franklin made the system better. When he was named Joint Postmaster General, he found new, shorter routes. Postriders also started traveling at night, which cut the time in half.

During wartime, mail delivery was very slow. Sometimes troops blocked the roads used by postmen. Sometimes ships carrying mail were captured by the British. Then letters were dumped overboard so that the enemy didn't discover any secrets.

Many people back then destroyed their letters. Abigail asked John to burn her letters too, but he didn't listen. Today, we know how women in the 1700s worked and lived—thanks to Abigail's letters.

▲ POSTMEN carried Abigail's mail by horseback.

ABIGAIL
Goes to Europe

Abigail was very lonely without her husband and oldest son at home. She tried to keep busy by earning extra money. She asked John to send her fans, handkerchiefs, and other items to sell in Braintree. Because of the war, Americans had a hard time finding these goods for a reasonable price. Abigail proved to be an excellent businesswoman.

Finally, on October 19, 1781, the British surrendered in Yorktown, Virginia. The war was over, but John was still needed in Europe. Abigail

▶ VICTORY! Britain's Lord Cornwallis surrenders to General George Washington at Yorktown, Virginia, in 1781.

grew more and more lonely over the next two years. John couldn't stand the separation either. So in 1783, when Congress offered him a job in Paris, he asked Abigail to join him.

Abigail was nervous. She had never been more than fifty miles from home! But she agreed to go. After tearful good-byes to friends and her sons Charles and Thomas, whom she was leaving behind, Abigail and Nabby boarded a ship called the *Active*. On June 20, 1784, the two women sailed for Europe.

A Long Journey

Abigail and Nabby brought trunks filled with clothes, dishes, and books. They also brought a cow, so they could have fresh milk. The journey was rough at first. Everyone got

▲ FRENCH PEOPLE had way too much fun for Abigail's tastes.

seasick. It didn't help that the ship was dirty and the food was terrible. However, Abigail soon took charge. She baked puddings and made sure the floors were scrubbed clean. The crew was pleased with Abigail's help.

The *Active* arrived safely in England on July 21. Abigail and Nabby were delighted to see John and John Quincy, who met them in London. After a happy reunion, the family went to France. Abigail thought the city of Paris was ugly, but she was pleased with their large home in the suburbs. It had a beautiful garden with orange trees and a fish pond.

Abigail bought a songbird to keep her company, since she didn't have many friends. (It didn't help that she couldn't speak the language.) She disliked the French, who had fun on Sunday instead of going to church. She also disliked many of the Americans she met in Paris—including Benjamin Franklin, whom she thought had poor manners. However, Abigail became good friends with Thomas Jefferson. They discussed politics and went sightseeing together.

After only nine months in Paris, the Adams family had to pack up. In the spring of 1785 John was named as the first United States ambassador to England. (Ambassadors represent their homeland in a foreign country.) Soon Abigail was on her way to a new adventure.

Life in London

Abigail was nervous about attending her first party in London. It was given by King George III and

KING GEORGE III (right) receives John Adams, America's first ambassador to Britain.

Queen Charlotte—whom the Americans had just fought in the war! Dressed in a fancy gown that she did not want to wear, Abigail felt silly waiting with two hundred people to meet the royal family. After four hours, it was finally her turn. She thought the king was kind, but she was not looking forward to any more parties at the palace.

The Adams family rented a house in London's Grosvenor Square. The city was expensive, and Abigail worried about how she would give parties without going broke. Luckily, before one important dinner, an American captain gave her a turtle that weighed 114 pounds! Abigail made turtle soup for everyone. The event was a success.

▼ GROSVENOR Square was a fashionable address in London.

Abigail liked sightseeing in London, but what she loved most were science lectures at the Royal Society. Women weren't allowed to attend such lectures in America. Abigail was disappointed when she was sick and had to miss a few.

▲ THE ROYAL SOCIETY in London, founded in 1660, is still active today.

Although Abigail was enjoying England, she missed her children back in the United States. She also missed politics. Thankfully, she and John would not be in London much longer. In the spring of 1788, the couple sailed home together to the land they both loved—America.

CAPITALS
and First Ladies

fter being greeted by a huge crowd at the Boston port, Abigail was eager to settle into their new home called Peacefield. This was a six-room house that John had bought before leaving London. Abigail thought

▲ **PEACEFIELD** is also known as the Old House. Four generations of the Adams family lived there from 1788 to 1927.

▲ JOHN attended the swearing-in of George Washington as president. It took place at Federal Hall in New York City, America's first capital.

it was small compared to the large homes in Europe. Yet the family wouldn't be living there much longer. The nation's first presidential elections were set for November 1788, and many people thought John might be chosen as vice president. They were right. John would serve under President George Washington to lead the new nation. Abigail was very proud of her husband.

The couple moved from Massachusetts to the nation's first capital, New York City, where they enjoyed dining with the president and his wife, Martha. Abigail and Martha Washington became good friends. The two women also shared several official duties, such as calling on visitors. In order to save time, Abigail would visit when she knew people weren't home, leaving a card with her name on it so they'd know she stopped by. That way, she could make many stops and spend more time with her family.

Abigail's social life got even busier in 1790, when the capital was moved to Philadelphia. She and John went to Braintree during the summers to relax. Two years later, Abigail fell ill and couldn't return to Philadelphia. When John was reelected as vice president in the fall, she stayed home for his entire term.

However, Abigail would soon have to move back to the capital city. In 1796 George Washington retired—and John was elected president. Abigail was going to be the nation's new First Lady.

Mrs. President

Unfortunately, Abigail couldn't attend John's inauguration ceremony. She needed to find someone to take care of the farm while she was away. While she was at home,

▲ AS FIRST LADY, Abigail hosted many parties and dinners.

she also tried to enroll a black farmhand named James in school. Parents complained, yet Abigail defended him. She believed that everyone should be educated— no matter what color or sex they were. In the end, James was allowed to go to school.

When Abigail finally returned to Philadelphia, she worried that she wouldn't be as popular as Martha Washington. Martha didn't talk much about politics. Abigail, on the other hand, liked to give her opinions and her advice to her husband. She was afraid her sharp tongue would get her in

▲ A SILK DRESS worn by Abigail Adams

Firsts for First Ladies

Without an example, Martha Washington and Abigail Adams had to decide how a First Lady should act. They had very different ideas. Martha entertained guests. Abigail helped her husband make decisions. Many First Ladies who followed them have done both. From Eleanor Roosevelt's press conferences to Jackie Kennedy's restoration of the White House, First Ladies have shown the world their opinions and styles. Nowadays they fight for their own causes as well, such as literacy and the environment.

In 1912, the Smithsonian Museum started displaying gowns worn by First Ladies. Today this popular exhibit also includes china, jewelry, invitations to parties, and campaign buttons.

trouble. It did. Abigail answered letters for John and defended his reputation. Some people thought she had too much power. They called her "Mrs. President."

Besides political struggles, Abigail and John had to deal with personal sorrow. Their son Charles drank too much and became very sick. He died in 1800, shortly after Abigail moved to the new capital city of Washington, D.C. The change of scenery did nothing to cheer her up. Washington was a mess. Mosquitoes were everywhere because the city had been built on a swamp. Hogs and cattle roamed the dirt roads. And

the President's Home—which would later become known as the White House—was far from finished. There was no paint on the walls and there was no furniture. Abigail had to hang her laundry in the East Room to dry.

Abigail would never get to spend much time in the White House. In the 1800 election, John was defeated by Thomas Jefferson. Abigail was disappointed. She knew that John would miss being involved in politics—and she would too. But at least they could soon retire to Peacefield together.

ABIGAIL was the first First Lady to live in the White House. She didn't like living there because it was cold and drafty.

A HAPPY
Retirement

A bigail may have missed being in politics, but she loved spending time with her children and grandchildren. She was thrilled when John Quincy and his wife, Louisa Catherine, finally came home from Europe, where they had lived for several years. Abigail was also glad that Thomas's family lived in Quincy. (Part of the town of Braintree had been renamed

◀ **GRANDMA ADAMS enjoyed her family but kept thinking and writing.**

Quincy in 1792, in honor of Abigail's grandfather.) Yet there were sad times too. In 1813, Nabby died of breast cancer—a rare disease back then. Abigail and John were heartbroken to lose their only daughter.

Family and friends were always important to Abigail. Many of them came to visit her as she lay on her deathbed, sick with typhoid fever. Thankfully, her illness was short and without much pain. Her last words of comfort to a sad John were, "Do not grieve, my friend, my dearest friend. I am ready to go. And John, it will not be long." She died on October 28, 1818, at the age of 73.

▼BARBARA BUSH is married to George H.W. Bush and is the mother of President George W. Bush. Along with John Adams and John Quincy Adams, the Bushes are the only father-son presidents.

► JOHN QUINCY, Abigail's son, went on to become a U.S. senator, secretary of state, and president of the United States.

Remembering Abigail

Sadly, Abigail did not live to see her son John Quincy become the sixth president of the United States. She would have been very proud of him. Abigail is one of only two women who had a husband *and* son become president. (The other is Barbara Bush, who is the wife of George Herbert Walker Bush and the mother of George W. Bush.)

Today, Abigail is remembered in many ways. Visitors can tour her childhood home, as well as the homes where she and John lived. The United First Parish Church in Quincy—where John,

◄ THIS STATUE of Abigail and John Quincy shows her pride in her son.

Abigail, John Quincy, and Louisa Catherine are all buried—is also open to the public. And Abigail is included in the Boston Women's Memorial, a series of sculptures celebrating three important women in the city's history.

Abigail Adams made many sacrifices so that America could survive. If John had kept working as a lawyer in Braintree, they could have had a comfortable life together. Yet they lived apart longer than any other Revolutionary War couple, because she knew how important it was for him to serve his country.

And, fortunately, Abigail's letter asking

Mystery Person

☞ CLUE 1: When I was born in 1820, women did not have the right to vote. I tried to change that by leading a movement.

☞ CLUE 2: In 1872, I was arrested for trying to vote in a presidential election. I refused to pay my $100 fine.

☞ CLUE 3: I never got to vote. I died in 1906—fourteen years before women won this important right.

Who am I?

SUSAN B. ANTHONY

▲ THE ADAMS houses, which are all part of the Adams National Historical Park, contain many rare objects. This library holds 14,000 books collected by the Adamses.

John to "Remember the Ladies" *was* remembered. Women in the twentieth century often quoted it as they fought for their rights. We can learn a lot from Abigail's willingness to speak her mind. Thanks to the brave words and actions of people like Abigail, we are able to live in a country where men— and women—are free.

▲ JOHN AND ABIGAIL'S burial place

THE BOSTON WOMEN'S MEMORIAL
has a statue of Abigail because she
was a force for justice and an
inspiration to others.

TALKING
About Abigail

▲ KELLY COBBLE

TIME For Kids editor Curtis Slepian spoke with Kelly Cobble about Abigail Adams. She is Curator of the Adams National Historical Park, in Quincy, Massachusetts.

Q: *Did Abigail influence John Adams?*

A: Yes. Sometimes John Adams lacked self-confidence. When he was down, she kept up his spirits. Abigail encouraged him to follow his heart and mind. She told him that it was okay not to be popular as long as he was honest with himself and others.

Abigail also influenced his ideas. She wanted him to use his education in history and law to deal with important issues that he faced as president. They both wanted equal rights and education for people. Only John was in a position to act on those ideas, but Abigail made sure to give him the woman's point of view.

▶ **FIRST FAMILIES First ladies and presidents (from left to right): Barbara Bush, George H. W. Bush, Lady Bird Johnson, Bill Clinton, Hillary Clinton, Gerald R. Ford, Betty Ford, Jimmy Carter, and Rosalynn Carter**

Q: *What is most inspiring about Abigail Adams?*
A: Abigail was ahead of her times. She favored laws protecting women's rights and believed that education for women would benefit women and their families. She spoke out against slavery and never owned slaves. And she often took care of her farm and family by herself.

Q: *How did Abigail influence the role of First Lady?*
A: Abigail sometimes stood in for the president during public ceremonies when he couldn't attend. It's a job first ladies still take on. Abigail gave her opinions to the press and tried to win over people to John's policies. Since then, first ladies have felt they could speak their mind.

Q: *What would be her message to kids today?*
A: Abigail gave this advice in a letter to her children. It probably still applies today: "Justice, Humanity and Benevolence are the duties you owe to society."

ABIGAIL ADAMS'S
Key Dates

1744	Born on October 11, in Weymouth, Massachusetts
1764	Marries John Adams
1775	Witnesses the Battle of Bunker Hill with John Quincy
1776	Writes her "Remember the Ladies" letter; hears the Declaration of Independence read in Boston
1784	Sails with Nabby to Europe
1789	Moves to New York City when John becomes vice president
1796	Becomes First Lady of the United States
1801	Retires with John at Peacefield
1818	Dies on October 28, in Quincy, Massachusetts

1755 The first dictionary, written by Englishman Samuel Johnson, is published.

1783 The Mongolfier brothers fly the first hot-air balloon, in Paris, France.

1804 Lewis and Clark explore the Northwest.